What DOGS Can Teach US

Inspiring Quotes & Beautiful Images

Julie Pallant

To the dogs who heal us — whether we meet them on the couch, at the park, or in the pages of a book.

Feeling stressed? Take a puppy break!

Studies show that even a few minutes spent looking at photos of adorable dogs can boost mood and lower stress levels. It turns out that our brains are wired to respond to "cute" — those big eyes and floppy ears trigger a rush of feel-good chemicals that make us calmer and happier.

The benefits are even more if you are lucky enough to own a dog! Patting a dog releases oxytocin, the hormone of trust and connection, while stress hormones like cortisol fade away. Your heart slows, your muscles relax, and suddenly the world feels a little softer around the edges.

Dogs are natural mindfulness teachers. They don't worry about yesterday or tomorrow — they're fully alive in every tail wag, walk, and treat. Spending time with them helps us do the same. Dog owners tend to walk more, laugh more, and feel less lonely. Even brief encounters — a pat in the park or a glance at a wagging tail — can lift a heavy mood.

So, whether you're scrolling through puppy pictures or sharing your couch with a loyal companion, dogs remind us that joy doesn't have to be complicated. Sometimes all it takes is four paws, a wet nose, and an open heart.

Ready for your daily dose of doggy therapy?
Turn the page and let your furry therapists put a smile on your face.

Julie Pallant

Therapist? I already have one — he drools, wags, and thinks I'm perfect.

Sometimes all you need is a friend who matches your vibe.

Dogs wake up every day believing something wonderful is about to happen — and it usually does.

The best gifts aren't wrapped—
they're furry, curious, and
full of joy.

Love means simply being there —
no advice, no fixing, just presence.

Dogs remind us that mindfulness begins with curiosity—start by noticing the world right beneath your nose.

Forgive quickly, nap often, and greet everyone like they matter.

Patience is a dog waiting at the door, tail thumping softly.

If only humans faced life's challenges with the same dignity as a dog forced to have a bath.

Find your joy and run straight toward it—ears flying, heart open, no hesitation.

A dog's birthday wish is simple:
more love, more walkies, and
maybe just one extra treat.

Stay balanced, stay brave, and never forget to enjoy the ride.

Every belly rub begins with trust —
and ends with joy.

Dogs teach us to stay curious, because there's always something beautiful waiting to be discovered.

The best kind of friends are the ones who race through life right beside you.

A dog doesn't fix what's broken — they simply make it easier to keep going.

Dogs remind us that joy doesn't come from having more — it comes from appreciating what's right in front of you.

Faith is waiting by the bowl and believing that love will fill it.

Confidence without arrogance, strength without aggression.

The world feels less overwhelming when you have someone beside you that loves you.

Dogs don't need clocks—they know that anytime is snack time.

Dogs may not read books, but they've mastered the chapters on love, loyalty, and living in the moment.

Dogs age the way we wish humans would—gracefully, honestly, without complaint.

Dogs remind us that listening is love in its quietest form.

love

Don't overthink joy:
just jump for it like a dog
after a frisbee.

We are braver together than we ever are alone.

Surround yourself with those who make you wag your tail.

Sometimes even the bravest hearts
need something soft to cuddle.

Self-care isn't selfish — it's how to stay *pawsitively* fabulous.

I may not understand everything you say, but I definitely understand snacks.

A greyhound's gift is knowing
when to sprint and when to be still
– a balance many of us are
still learning.

There's no such thing as too many puppies—just too few arms to hold them.

Some problems require action. Others require a cosy blanket and a glass of red.

Images and words by Julie Pallant (PhD)

As a photographer, I love capturing real dogs, but anyone who has tried to photograph their own pet knows how unpredictable they can be. For this book, I wanted images that perfectly matched the mood of each quote, and some of these scenes would be almost impossible to create in real life.

AI allowed me to design thoughtful, expressive images that reflect the spirit of dogs in a way that was engaging. Although AI has attracted a lot of criticism, I have found it to be a useful creative tool that helps produce beautiful visuals capable of bringing a little joy to the day.

Want more information about how I created the images in this book using AI?

On my website I have created a blog explaining how I created the images presented in this book using AI. If you would like to learn how to do this yourself scan the QR with your phone or follow the links provided at:

https://linktr.ee/jpallant

What Dogs Can Teach Us: Inspiring Quotes & Beautiful Images

Copyright © 2025 Julie Pallant
First edition 2025

All rights reserved. No part of this publication may be reproduced, stored in a retrieval system, or transmitted in any form or by any means—electronic, mechanical, photocopying, recording, or otherwise—without the prior written permission of the publisher, except in the case of brief quotations used in reviews or articles. Every effort has been made to ensure that the information in this book is accurate. However, this book is intended as a source of inspiration and reflection only. The author and publisher disclaim any liability arising directly or indirectly from the use of this book.

Images and text: © Julie Pallant

Design and layout: Images, words, design and layout by Julie Pallant

Publisher: Pallant Creative Solutions julie@pallantcreativesolutions.com

A catalogue record for this book is available from the National Library of Australia

ISBN (Paperback): 978-0-6453476-2-3

For information about this and other titles by Julie Pallant, visit the link provided at https://linktr.ee/jpallant.
Contact Julie Pallant by email at julie@juliepallant.com.au

www.ingramcontent.com/pod-product-compliance
Lightning Source LLC
Chambersburg PA
CBHW042044290426
44109CB00001B/27